For Milly, Oscar, and all little explorers
MB

For Eva, Iván, and Olov
JV

First US edition 2021

Library of Congress Catalog Card Number 2021934426
ISBN 978-1-5362-1723-0

APS 26 25 24 23
10 9 8 7 6 5

Printed in Humen, Dongguan, China

This book was typeset in Berylium.
The illustrations were created digitally.

Candlewick Press
99 Dover Street
Somerville, Massachusetts 02144

www.candlewick.com

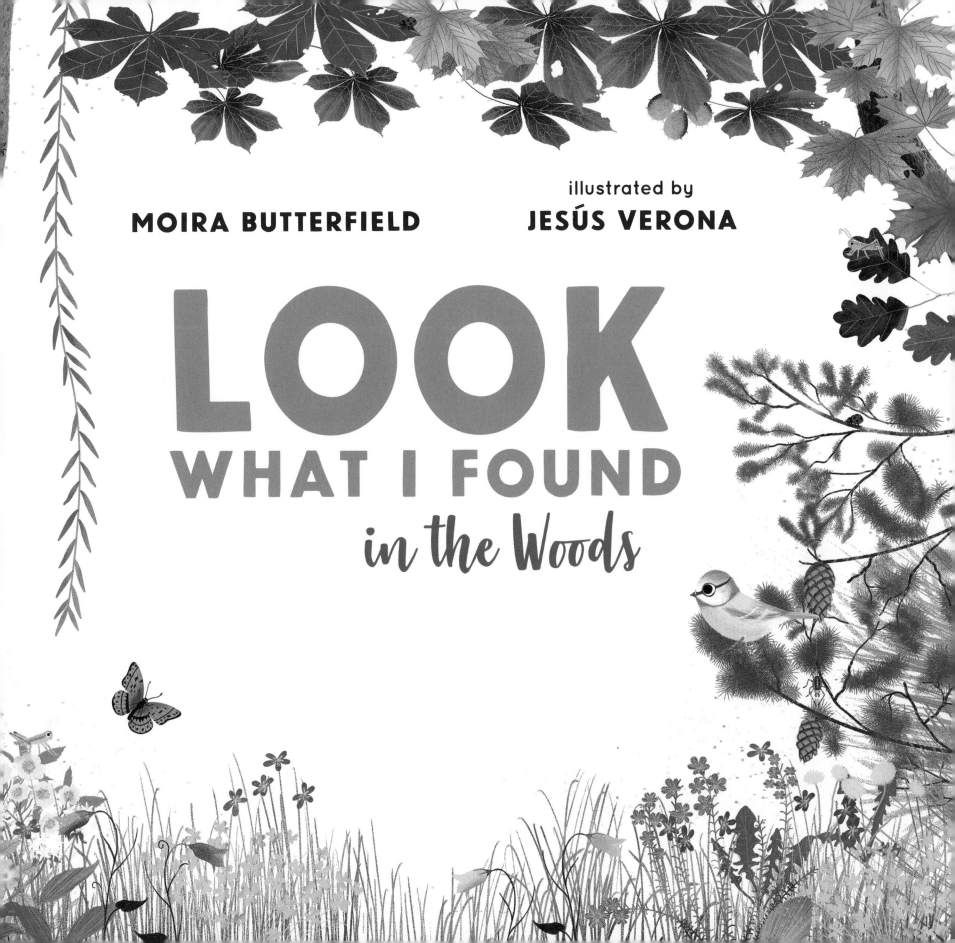

MOIRA BUTTERFIELD

illustrated by **JESÚS VERONA**

LOOK
WHAT I FOUND
in the Woods

Follow me. I know the way.
We're walking through the woods today.

Look what I found!
A curly stick that looks like a magic wand.

WOODS

Can you also find . . .
- one signpost to show the way?
- two butterflies fluttering?
- three bright-yellow flowers?

A tree's branches and leaves are called its crown. Crowns grow in different shapes and sizes.

Some are tall and pointy . . .

and some spread out wide.

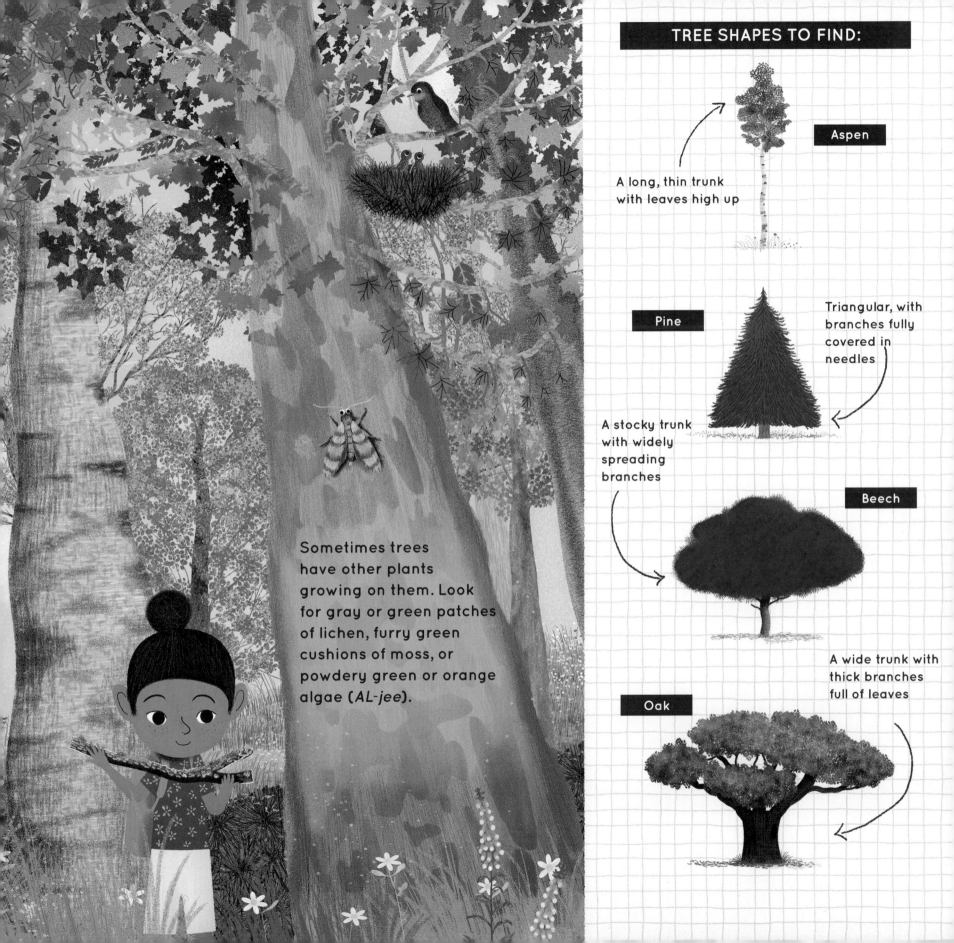

Sometimes trees have other plants growing on them. Look for gray or green patches of lichen, furry green cushions of moss, or powdery green or orange algae (*AL-jee*).

TREE SHAPES TO FIND:

Aspen

A long, thin trunk with leaves high up

Pine

Triangular, with branches fully covered in needles

A stocky trunk with widely spreading branches

Beech

A wide trunk with thick branches full of leaves

Oak

Let's look at the trees up close . . .
Which ones will we like the most?

Look what I found!

Trees covered in rough bark to
make a rubbing on.

Can you also find . . .

- one twiggy bird's nest?
- two squirrels racing?
- three busy bumblebees?

Some trees make a sticky resin that seeps out of their bark like dollops of glue. It is full of chemicals that keep insects away. It can also make people sick, so it's best not to touch it.

Bark is a hard outer layer that protects the inside of a tree from weather, animals, and even other plants.

Trees sometimes have holes in their bark where a branch once grew. Animals such as squirrels and birds often use the holes to build their nests in.

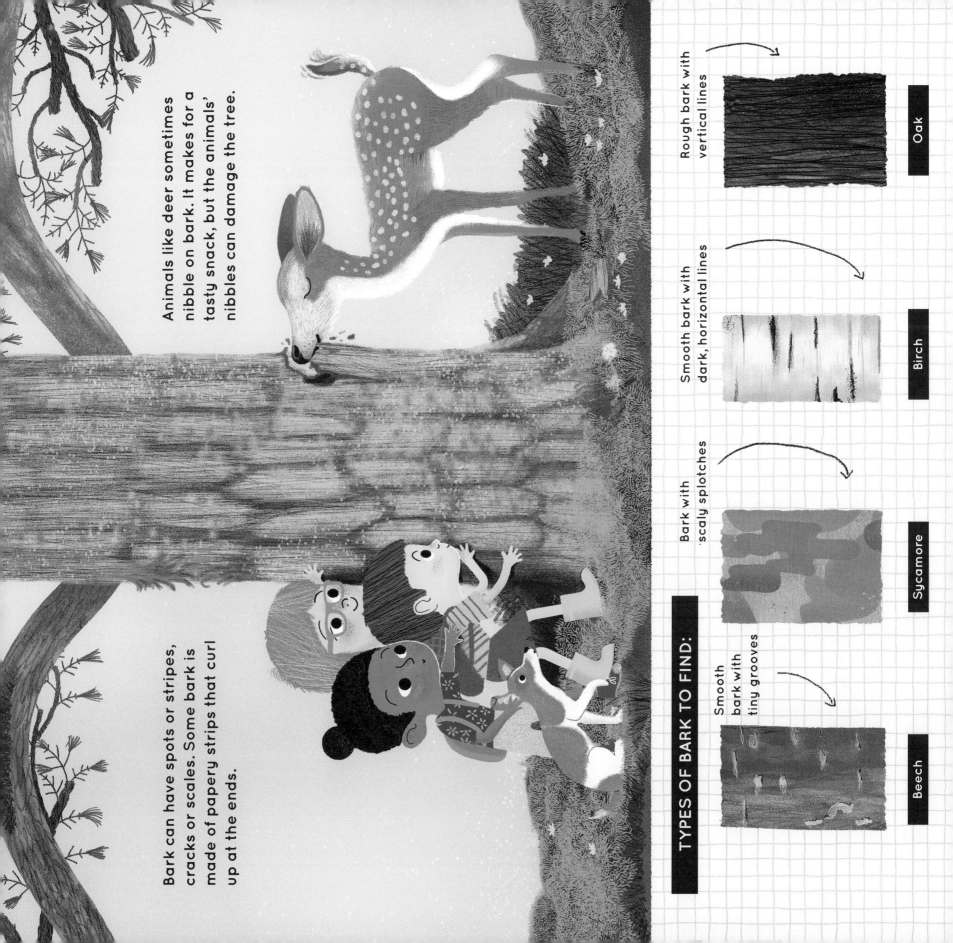

Animals like deer sometimes nibble on bark. It makes for a tasty snack, but the animals' nibbles can damage the tree.

Bark can have spots or stripes, cracks or scales. Some bark is made of papery strips that curl up at the ends.

TYPES OF BARK TO FIND:

Rough bark with vertical lines

Oak

Smooth bark with dark, horizontal lines

Birch

Bark with scaly splotches

Sycamore

Smooth bark with tiny grooves

Beech

Finding treasure from the trees,
blown down by the rustling breeze.

Look what I found!
Two leaves that make fun bunny ears.

Can you also find . . .
- one robin hopping?
- two lacy spiderwebs?
- three little purple flowers?

Leaves are an important part of a tree. They use sunlight to make a sugary food, called glucose, which helps the tree grow.

If you hold a thin leaf up to the light, you might be able to see tiny lines inside it. These lines are called veins. They carry water from the leaf's stem to the whole leaf. They also carry the food the leaf makes back to the stem. From there it travels to the rest of the tree.

Some trees have leaves that are known as needles. Because the needles stay on the branches all year long, these types of trees are called evergreen trees.

LEAF SHAPES TO FIND:

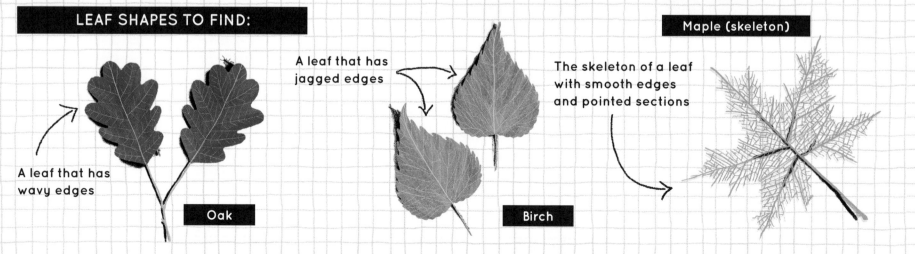

A leaf that has jagged edges

The skeleton of a leaf with smooth edges and pointed sections

Maple (skeleton)

A leaf that has wavy edges

Oak

Birch

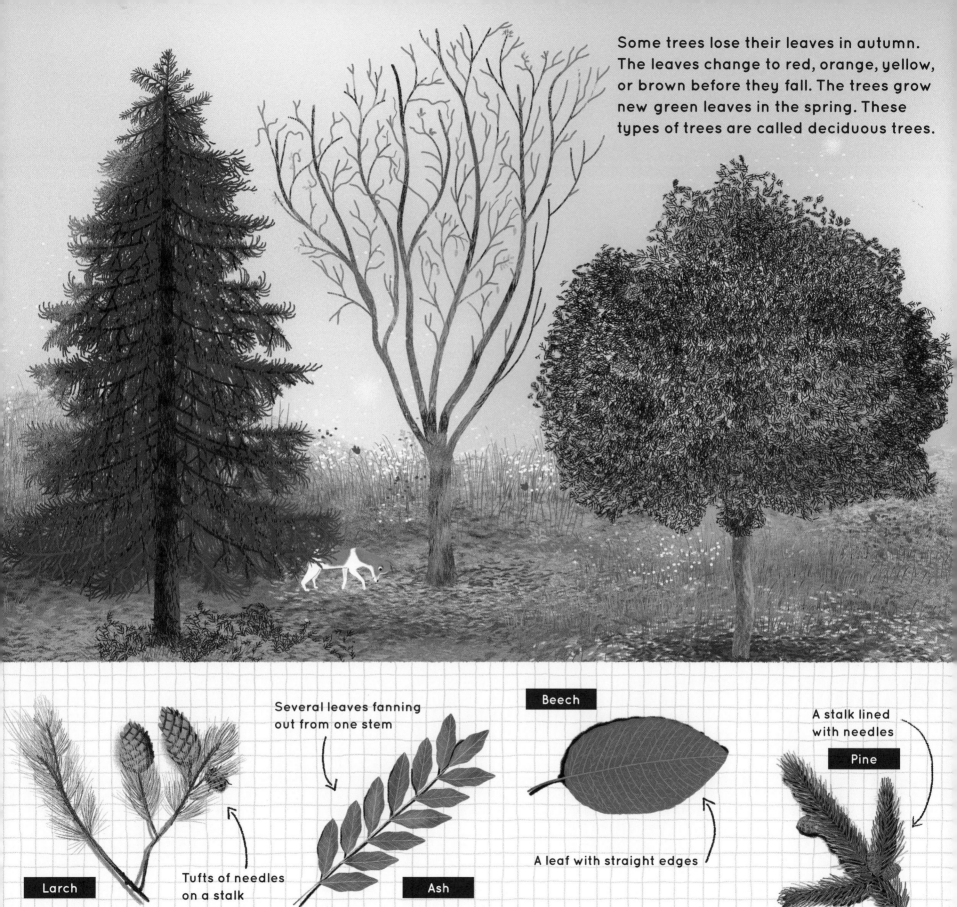

Some trees lose their leaves in autumn. The leaves change to red, orange, yellow, or brown before they fall. The trees grow new green leaves in the spring. These types of trees are called deciduous trees.

Larch

Tufts of needles on a stalk

Several leaves fanning out from one stem

Ash

Beech

A leaf with straight edges

A stalk lined with needles

Pine

Hunting underneath a tree,
what small secrets do we see?

Look what I found!
A seed like a tiny helicopter.

Can you also find ...
- one big blackbird?
- two crawling centipedes?
- three tiny wild strawberries?

Some trees grow their seeds inside hard casings called nuts. When they are ready to germinate, the nuts fall to the ground. They can be gathered for food by animals and people.

Other trees grow their seeds inside soft fruit, such as apples and pears.

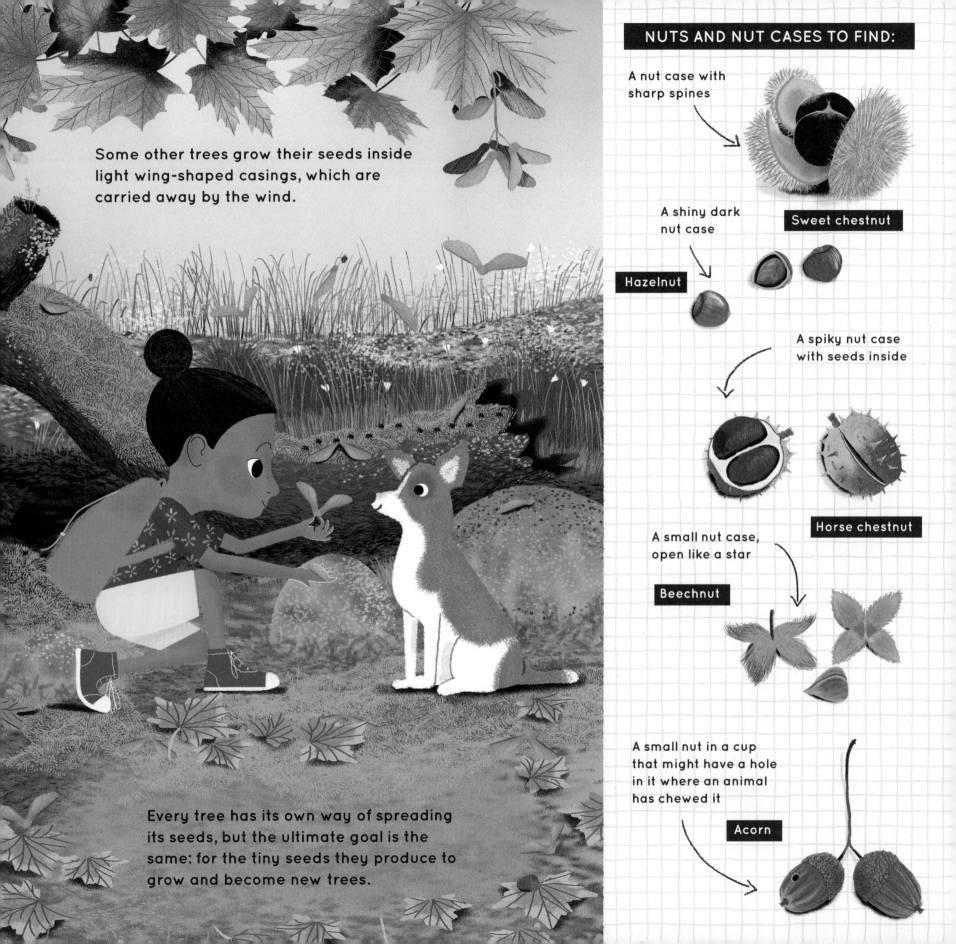

Some other trees grow their seeds inside light wing-shaped casings, which are carried away by the wind.

Every tree has its own way of spreading its seeds, but the ultimate goal is the same: for the tiny seeds they produce to grow and become new trees.

NUTS AND NUT CASES TO FIND:

A nut case with sharp spines

Sweet chestnut

A shiny dark nut case

Hazelnut

A spiky nut case with seeds inside

Horse chestnut

A small nut case, open like a star

Beechnut

A small nut in a cup that might have a hole in it where an animal has chewed it

Acorn

Searching in the woodland shade,
finding things the trees have made.

Look what I found!
A pine cone with its scales
stretched open like petals.

Can you also find . . .
- one birdhouse where birds can nest?
- two black crows?
- three pink flowers?

Some trees, called conifers, grow hard cones to protect their seeds. The seeds are tucked safely under the scales of the cone.

When the weather is cold or damp, the cone's scales close to protect the seeds within.

The smallest cones are as small as a thumb, but the biggest ones can be as large as a football.

When the weather gets warm and dry, the cone's scales open and the seeds fall out, ready to grow into new trees.

CONE SHAPES TO FIND:

A big round cone with open scales

Bristlecone

Aleppo pine

A long, thin cone

A bunch of mini cones

Alder

A short, fat cone

Larch

Fallen logs with holes inside,
where little creatures like to hide.

Look what I found!

A swirly, striped snail shell.

Can you also find . . .

- one slimy black slug?
- two ladybugs?
- three shiny black beetles?

A snail carries its home on its back. It can curl up and disappear inside its shell to hide from predators.

Be sure to only collect empty shells, so as not to harm any snails.

Snails and slugs eat leaves and bark, so the woods are a great place for them to find a meal.

Beetles often crawl inside dead logs and munch on the rotting wood.

When animals eat dead wood and leaves, they are contributing to the cycle of life. They are like tiny recycling trucks, reusing the wood for their food.

Lots of woodland animals hunt smaller creatures and insects to eat.

SNAIL SHELLS TO FIND:

A tiny shell that's round and flat

A shell with dark and light stripes

A shell that looks transparent like glass

A shell that's shaped like a cone

Goodbye, woods.
We're homeward bound.

Look at all the things we've found . . .

TREASURE!

As you collect, be thoughtful, too.
Bring no harm with what you do.

When you're exploring the woods, only collect things that you find on the ground.
Never pick from trees or flowers or do anything that could harm animals.
This helps ensure that the woods will stay beautiful and healthy for future visits.